TOWNSHIP OF UNION
FREE PUBLIC LIBRARY
P9-CMT-460

Rookie Read-About™ Science

What's Your Favorite Flower?

By Allan Fowler

Consultants:
Robert L. Hillerich, Ph.D., Bowling Green State University, Bowling Green, Ohio

Mary Nalbandian, Director of Science, Chicago Public Schools, Chicago, Illinois

Fay Robinson, Child Development Specialist

CHILDRENS PRESS®
CHICAGO

Design by Beth Herman Design Associates

Library of Congress Cataloging-in-Publication Data

Fowler, Allan
What's your favorite flower? / by Allan Fowler.
p. cm. –(Rookie read-about science)
Summary: Illustrations and simple text describe various kinds of flowers and how they grow.
ISBN 0-516-06007-4
1. Flowers–Juvenile literature. [1. Flowers.] I. Title.
II. Series: Fowler, Allan. Rookie read-about science.
SB406.5.F68 1992
635.9–dc20 92-7404
CIP
AC

Printed in the United States of America.
1 2 3 4 5 6 7 8 9 10 R 00 99 98 97 96 95 94 93 92

Don't you feel a little
happier when there
are beautiful flowers
to look at and to smell?

You can find many kinds of flowers in many bright colors in the springtime.

Daisies and daffodils,
pansies and petunias,

marigolds, morning glories, and hundreds more!

Roses are among the
best-loved flowers.

Some people plant gardens with nothing but different types of roses.

Sometimes you can guess the color of a flower by its name —

like the bluebell, violet, buttercup, or snowdrop.

Besides the flowers that
people plant, there are
flowers that grow wild
in the countryside, on
mountains, in the woods,
and near the seashore.

You can even find flowers in the desert — on cactus plants.

When you look at a flower, the first thing you see is the petals.

They are brightly colored and smell sweet.

Other parts of a flower are the stamens with their dusty pollen and the pistil.

Under the petals is a bulging area. This is where the seeds are stored.

New plants can grow from seeds if they have soil, sunlight, and water.

A flowering plant will grow flower buds.

This bud is ready to blossom into a beautiful flower.

Some other flowers, like tulips, grow from bulbs instead of seeds.

Flowers grow on many
kinds of plants.

Some plants are almost
all flowers.

Some flowers grow on bushes, like lilacs, with their fresh, sweet scent.

Some grow on trees, like these beautiful cherry blossoms.

Every state in the United States and every province in Canada has its own special flower.

Many people have favorite flowers, too. Do you?

Words You Know

seeds

buds

bulbs

flowers

daisy

daffodils

bluebells

rose

morning glory

marigolds

snowdrops

tulips

lilacs

Index

About the Author

Allan Fowler is a free-lance writer with a background in advertising. Born in New York, he lives in Chicago now and enjoys traveling.

Photo Credits

PhotoEdit – ©David Young-Wolff, 3,23,30 (bottom right); ©Tony Freeman, 17, 30 (top right); ©Michael Newman, 20; ©Myrleen Ferguson, 29

Superstock International, Inc. – ©Manfred Thonig, Cover

Valan – ©Kennon Cooke, 4, 9, 28, 31 (bottom center); ©Tom W. Parkin, 5; ©Harold V. Green, 6, 13, 21, 30 (center right), 31 (top left); ©V. Wilkinson, 6 (inset), 31 (top center); ©Gerhard Kahrmann, 7 (2 photos), 26, 31 (center center, center right, bottom right); ©Michael J. Johnson, 10, 31 (top right); ©Herman H. Giethoorn, 11, 31 (bottom left); ©Jeff Foott, 14, 15; ©Hälle Flygare, 18, 30 (left); ©Wayne Lankinen, 19; ©J.R. Page, 22; ©Mildred McPhee, 25

COVER: Keukenho Gardens, Lisse, Netherlands